YOUR SKIN FACTORY

A production manual for better skin

Written by **Dr. Des Fernandes** MB, BCH, FRCS (Edin) & **Jennifer Munro**

Fernro Publishers Ltd. 2013

First published September 2013
Fernro Publishing Ltd.
London
United Kingdom

ISBN 978-0-9576681-1-9

Credits:
Kim Benvenuto for design and layout
Dr Sarah Lawson for editing
All photographs are used with the permission of
Environ Skin Care (Pty) Ltd.

www.yourskinfactory.com

You are your own **Factory Manager**: you are in charge of the buildings, machinery, supply of raw materials, health and safety, staff, production, security, repairs, maintenance and future development of your Skin Factory.

It's your job to ensure quality so that your factory runs as smoothly as possible; producing beautiful, healthy skin throughout your life.

Welcome to:

YOUR SKIN FACTORY

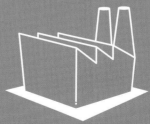

Your Skin Factory

01 **Sample and Works Order**

03 **Production Manual**

07 **Factory Structure**

09 **Detailed Factory Structure**

17 **Staff**

21 **Machinery**

23 **Raw Materials**

27 **Normal Delivery**

→

Department 1 – Quality Control 31

Department 2 – Maintenance 61

Department 3 – Health and Safety 65

Department 4 – Post-production Repairs and Improvements 67

Department 5 – Post Production Repairs and Improvements: luxury mode 81

An appointment with the Doctor 87

About the Authors 95

THE WORKS ORDER

01

WORKS ORDER FOR YOUR SKIN FACTORY

Customer name: *Myself*

Product: *New skin every day*

Specification:

- *Soft, smooth, even-coloured, waterproof and healthy.*
- *Not too thin or too thick, too oily or too dry; too tight or too loose.*
- *Keep germs and harmful chemicals out.*
- *Heal quickly, if breached.*
- *It must not itch or feel uncomfortable.*
- *Protect the inner organs, and deflect harmful rays.*
- *Anchor the hair*
- *Allow feelings of pleasure and warn of danger.*
- *Keep the body at a comfortable temperature.*
- *Skin to last a lifetime!*
- *N.B. Customer specifically does not want spots, acne, wrinkles, rashes, redness, dryness or pigmentation*

THE MASTER PLAN:

- All forms of life on earth have a DNA plan.

- Your DNA is the original genetic plan that decides what colour your skin should be, how thick it should be, how resistant to sun damage and how hairy it should be, as well as many other things.

- You are born with this master plan in place.

- The master plan is for your skin to be as perfect as listed on the works order specification for the Skin Factory.

- DNA is a chemical molecule.

- It can be damaged (you'll learn how later).

- When the DNA plan is damaged you get loss of internal quality control, faults in policing and not only that, but also deviations from the Master Plan – and that's when the problems arise.

" THIS IS THE COMPLEX, MAGICAL CHEMICAL SPIRAL THAT REPRESENTS THE DNA MOLECULE "

The two main threads are connected to each other by rungs composed of two special chemicals called nucleotides. There are only four nucleotides (represented by the yellow-blue and green-red "rungs") that bind to each other in an unvarying pattern – green always binds to red, and blue always binds to yellow. The arrangement of these nucleotides creates the code the makes up a gene.

This amazing spiral carries billions of rungs and if all the DNA of an average adult human body were laid out in a long thread, then this thread would go from earth to the sun and back seventy times. No computer would be able to compress information that efficiently.

**SHOWROOM AND SURFACE
ALTERNATIVE RECEIVING BAY
OR THE HORNY LAYER**

**FACTORY FLOOR
OR THE EPIDERMIS**

**BASEMENT ADMINISTRATION /
DEEP RECEIVING BAY
OR BASAL LAYER OF THE EPIDERMIS**

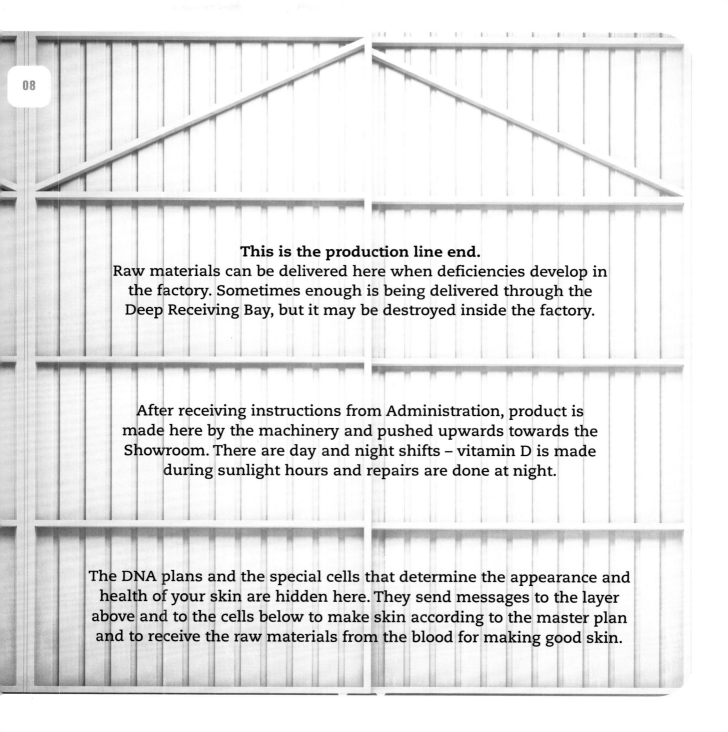

This is the production line end.
Raw materials can be delivered here when deficiencies develop in the factory. Sometimes enough is being delivered through the Deep Receiving Bay, but it may be destroyed inside the factory.

After receiving instructions from Administration, product is made here by the machinery and pushed upwards towards the Showroom. There are day and night shifts – vitamin D is made during sunlight hours and repairs are done at night.

The DNA plans and the special cells that determine the appearance and health of your skin are hidden here. They send messages to the layer above and to the cells below to make skin according to the master plan and to receive the raw materials from the blood for making good skin.

BASEMENT & ADMINISTRATION CENTRE

The Basement Admin area stores the individual plans for your Skin Factory; called DNA.

It's the very essence of you! It is what determines your colouring, shape, size and many other things.

The DNA lies inside the Stem cell factories that make skin cells, and also in the Fibroblasts that make Collagen and Elastin in the very basement area below the epidermis.

Your unique DNA plan is kept here in the basement admin.

"DAMAGE TO THE ADMIN AREA IS FAR MORE SERIOUS THAN DAMAGE TO THE SHOWROOM

PROTECT YOUR DNA PLAN

IT MAKES YOU WHAT YOU ARE"

PRODUCTION ON THE FACTORY FLOOR

Structure of the Epidermis

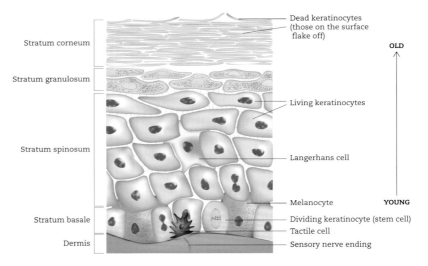

Stratum corneum

Stratum granulosum

Stratum spinosum

Stratum basale

Dermis

Dead keratinocytes (those on the surface flake off)

OLD

Living keratinocytes

Langerhans cell

Melanocyte

YOUNG

Dividing keratinocyte (stem cell)

Tactile cell

Sensory nerve ending

Skin Cell Machines – Keratinocytes and Keratinocyte Stem Cells

The Keratinocytes consult the DNA plan, take the raw materials, and turn them into new skin for you.

The new skin is pushed upwards towards the Showroom area (Horny layer or surface).

In this very clever factory the Keratinocyte Stem Cell Machines make new machines!

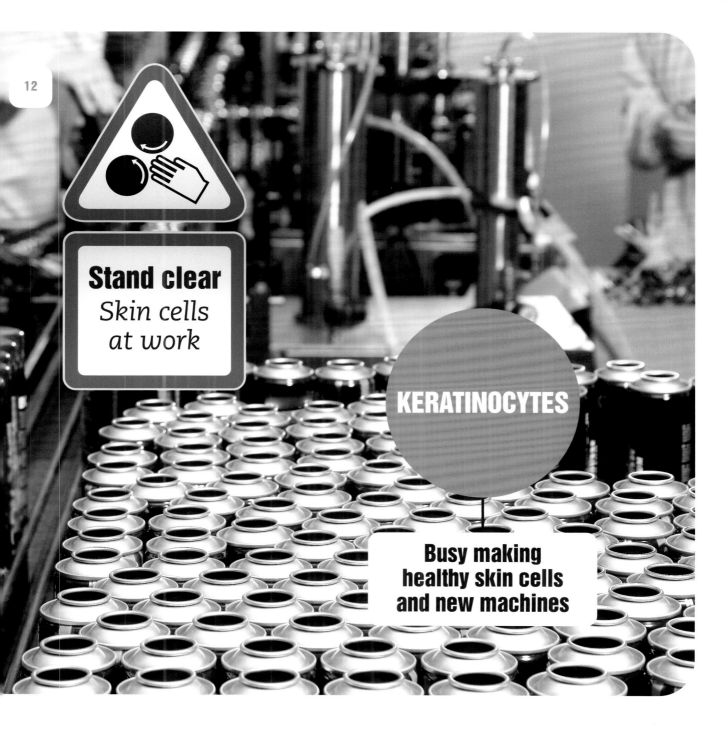

Stand clear
*Skin cells
at work*

KERATINOCYTES

**Busy making
healthy skin cells
and new machines**

THE PAINT BOOTH – COLOUR CENTRE

PAINT BOOTH – MELANOCYTES

The Melanocytes receive information from your DNA and choose the right colours for your Skin Factory.

When the Admin Area (DNA) is damaged, it sends wonky messages to the Paint Booth, and bad pigmentation marks are the result.

I hope I mixed this colour exactly right...

"YOUR PAINT BOOTH NEEDS **ACCURATE COLOUR REFERENCES** FROM THE ADMIN CENTRE TO GET YOUR SKIN COLOUR **JUST RIGHT** AND **MAINTAIN IT** ACCORDING TO THE STANDARDS OF **THE MASTER PLAN**"

THE SHOWROOM AND ALTERNATIVE RECEIVING BAY

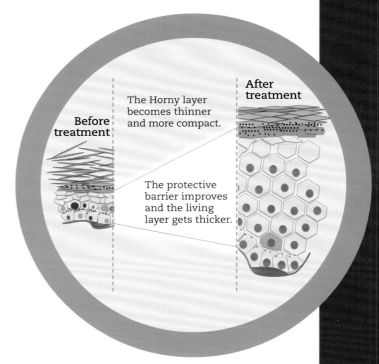

Before treatment

After treatment

The Horny layer becomes thinner and more compact.

The protective barrier improves and the living layer gets thicker.

The final product in the Showroom can be healthy and plump, or sad and thin, depending on raw ingredients and the health of the machinery below.

Does your machinery need repairs or maintenance?

Raw Materials can also be loaded into the Factory through the Horny layer / Alternative Receiving Bay.

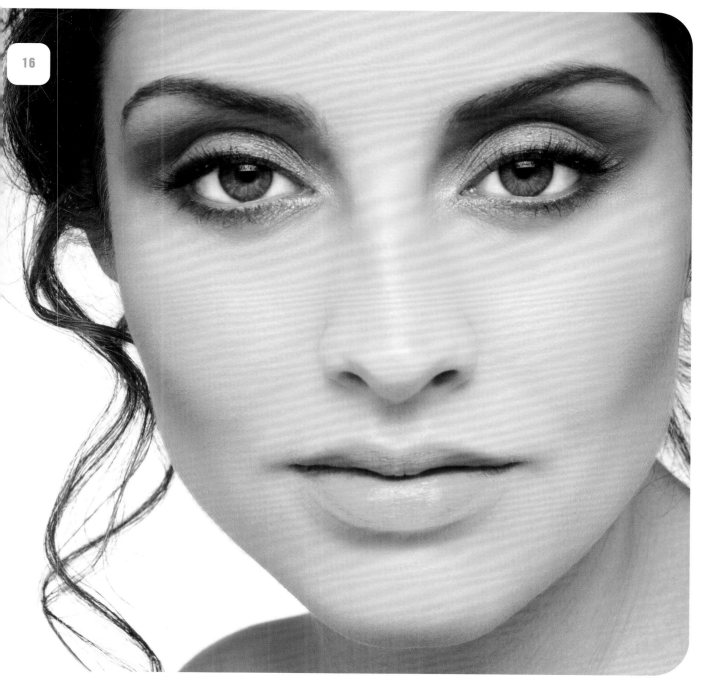

16

© Environ

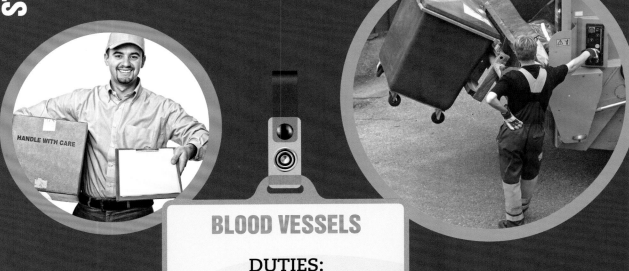

BLOOD VESSELS

DUTIES:
Deliveries
Waste Removal

Note: Blood vessels supply the skin cells with nutrients, water and oxygen, and remove waste. Cells die when these vital services stop, i.e. when you smoke, starve or eat junk food.

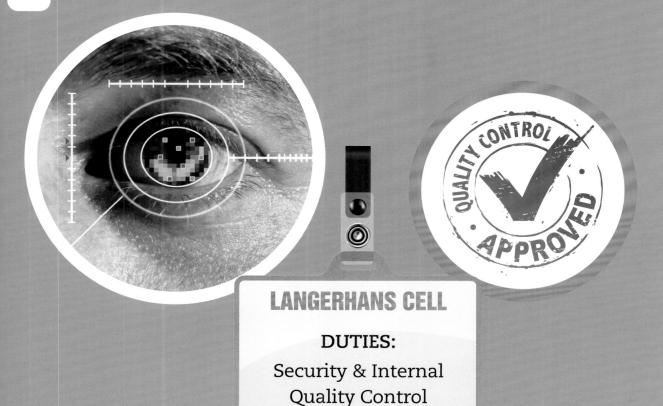

LANGERHANS CELL

DUTIES:
Security & Internal
Quality Control

The Langerhans cell makes sure that attacks on the factory are resisted and that the Master Plan for each cell is not altered. Unfortunately, the defensive plans can go wrong when this cell is attacked by sunlight, pollution or smoking, because then the Langerhans cells become ineffective.

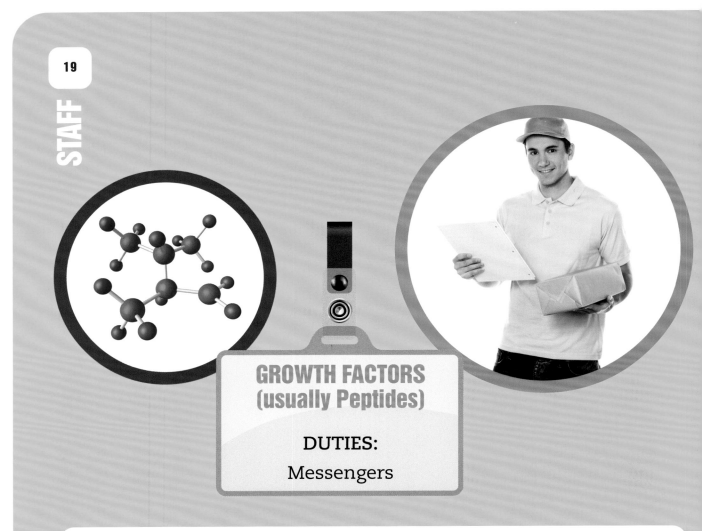

GROWTH FACTORS
(usually Peptides)

DUTIES:

Messengers

Growth factors, which are usually Peptides, act as messengers between the cells and tell the machinery to get on with the job of making skin cells, Elastin and Collagen.

YOUR SKIN FACTORY PRODUCES ITS BEST PRODUCT WHEN THE WHOLE TEAM WORKS TOGETHER

YOUR SKIN FACTORY'S MACHINES ARE SKIN CELLS:

The *Basal Keratinocytes* determine the epidermal thickness and effectiveness.

The *Melanocytes* determine the colour of the skin.

The *Fibroblasts* produce Collagen and Elastin fibres, making skin firm and youthful looking. They also make the jelly (glycoseaminoglycans) that these fibres lie in to give it a plump appearance.

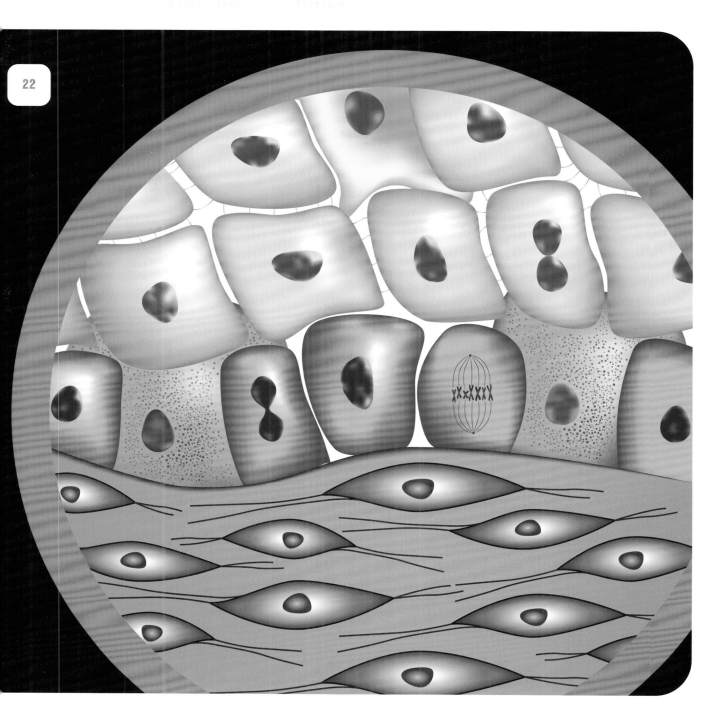

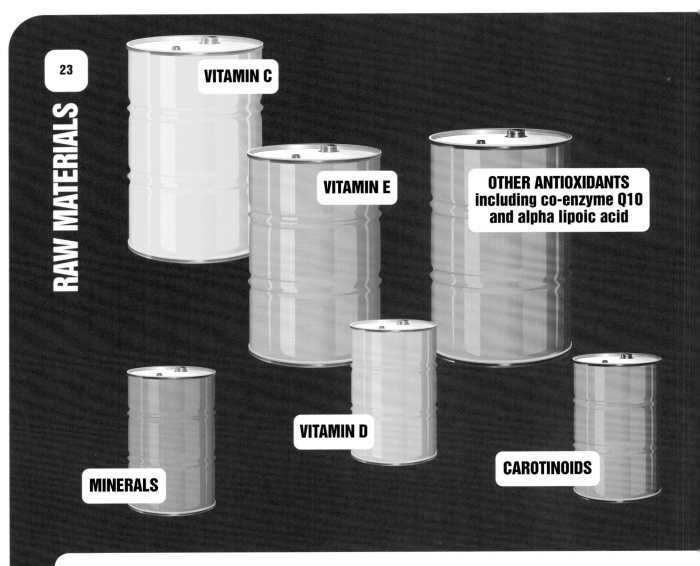

RAW MATERIALS

VITAMIN C

VITAMIN E

OTHER ANTIOXIDANTS
including co-enzyme Q10
and alpha lipoic acid

VITAMIN D

CAROTINOIDS

MINERALS

All of these raw ingredients are essential for healthy skin that conforms to the DNA plan; however, none of them is as important as vitamin A.

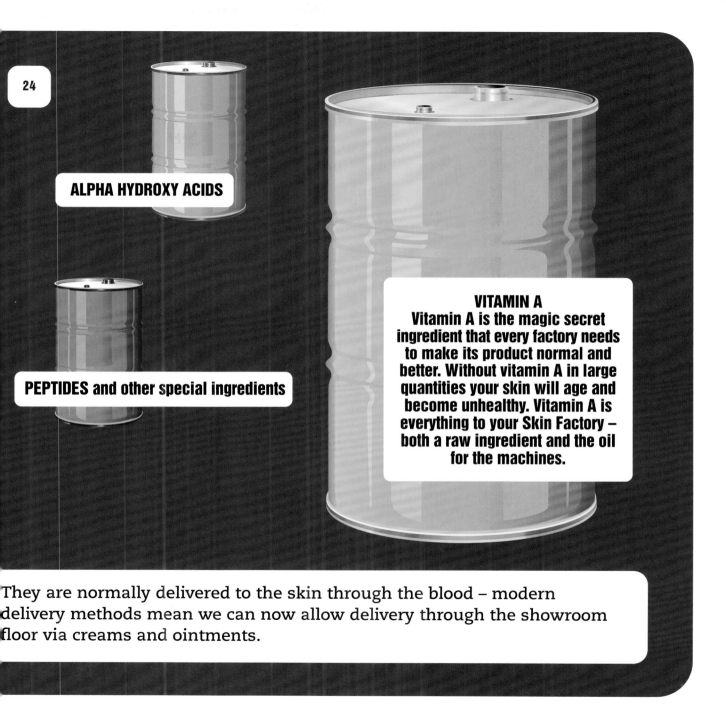

24

ALPHA HYDROXY ACIDS

PEPTIDES and other special ingredients

VITAMIN A
Vitamin A is the magic secret ingredient that every factory needs to make its product normal and better. Without vitamin A in large quantities your skin will age and become unhealthy. Vitamin A is everything to your Skin Factory – both a raw ingredient and the oil for the machines.

They are normally delivered to the skin through the blood – modern delivery methods mean we can now allow delivery through the showroom floor via creams and ointments.

"SUPPLY THE FACTORY WITH THE RAW INGREDIENTS IT NEEDS TO PERFORM AT ITS PEAK"

That makes sense, doesn't it?

You have to be the Chief Buyer for your own Skin Factory...

Where do you find these Raw Materials?

- In healthy food
- In good quality supplements
- In cosmeceutical creams and gels*

NOTE TO CHIEF BUYER

Ensure the creams you buy have effective active ingredients (check for date stamps – *the fresher the better!!*), and only buy airless dispensers or laminated aluminium foil tubes – not tubs where germs can breed, and active molecules can be degraded by exposure to light and air!

For new users of vitamin A creams, buy a lower dose and gradually build up to the higher doses.**

Preservative-free is an extra bonus!

* A cross between cosmetics and pharmaceuticals. The law prevents real Cosmeceutics from being called pharmaceuticals.

** It should receive low doses of vitamin A to help normalise it, and then go on to higher doses to reverse damage. Damaged skin loses its ability to use vitamin A normally.

"YOUR SKIN FACTORY WAS DESIGNED TO RECEIVE RAW MATERIALS FROM FOOD, THROUGH THE BLOOD VESSELS **BUT...** THINGS DON'T ALWAYS WORK AS THEY SHOULD"

Your Skin Factory has to use its Alternative or Surface Receiving Bay too – this means creams, oils and gels!

NORMAL DELIVERY

→ **Important** molecules like **vitamin A** require special gates to enter the cell.

→ Another set of gates is needed to allow vitamin A to enter the nucleus area where the **DNA** is.

→ These gates are like delivery **security checks.**

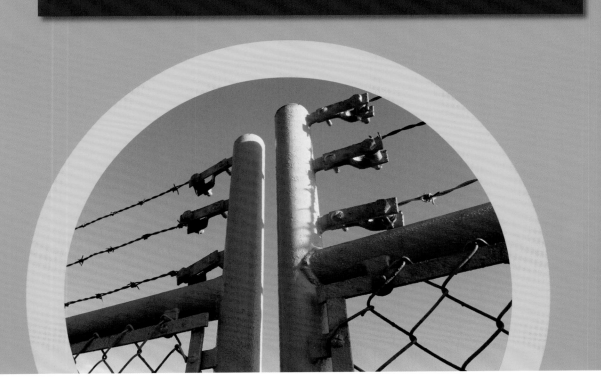

→ When skin has been deprived of vitamin A these gates start to disappear.

→ **Sunlight** encourages them to disappear.

→ Vitamin A itself is the stimulus to make more gates.

→ When we first start to stock up the raw ingredients of the factory, we have to use controlled lower doses of vitamin A, until enough gates have been opened for the vitamin A to enter the cell.

→ If the gates aren't there, then the vitamin A accumulates outside the cell, where it is not supposed to be, and **causes irritation.**

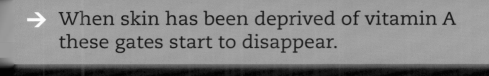

"YOU ARE YOUR OWN EXTERNAL QUALITY CONTROLLER!

CHECK THE WORKS ORDER AND THE SAMPLE

WE CALL SKIN THAT CONFORMS 'NORMAL SKIN'**"

*** You can afford to do no more than simple Maintenance to Normal Skin.*

" **SKIN THAT DOESN'T CONFORM TO THE WORKS ORDER AND SAMPLE IS DEFECTIVE AND MUST BE 'NORMALISED' USING SUPPLEMENTS AND CREAMS** "

FACTORY DEFECTS:

1. Photo–ageing / Free radical activity

Wrinkles
Excess Pigmentation
Redness
Dryness
Sagging
Altered DNA

2. Disease

Skin Cancer
Eczema
Acne
Rashes
Psoriasis
Etc.

"

LINES AND WRINKLES **ARE ALL IMPROVED** WITH **VITAMIN A** AND **ANTIOXIDANTS** **IN HIGH-DOSE** SUPPLEMENTS & CREAMS

"

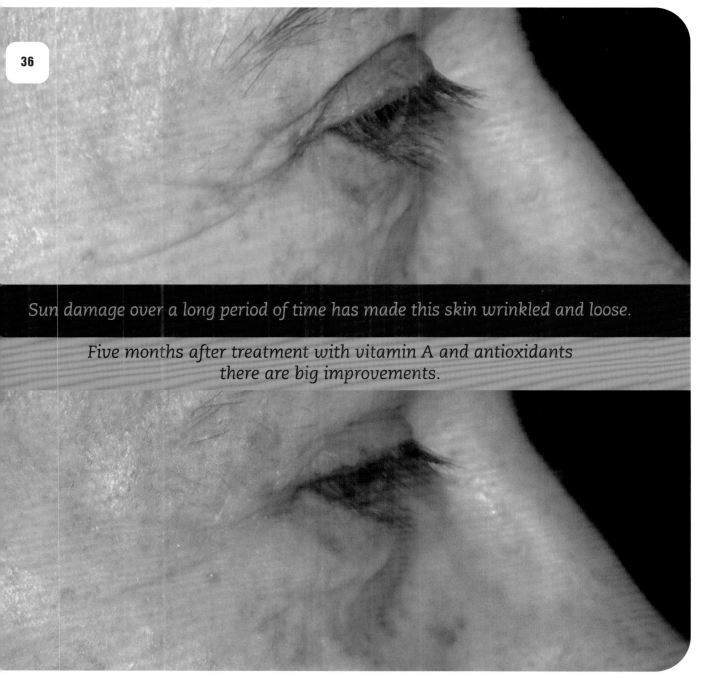

36

Sun damage over a long period of time has made this skin wrinkled and loose.

Five months after treatment with vitamin A and antioxidants there are big improvements.

© Environ

Dept #1. QUALITY CONTROL

"
EVEN SEVERE
SUN DAMAGE
CAN BE
IMPROVED
"

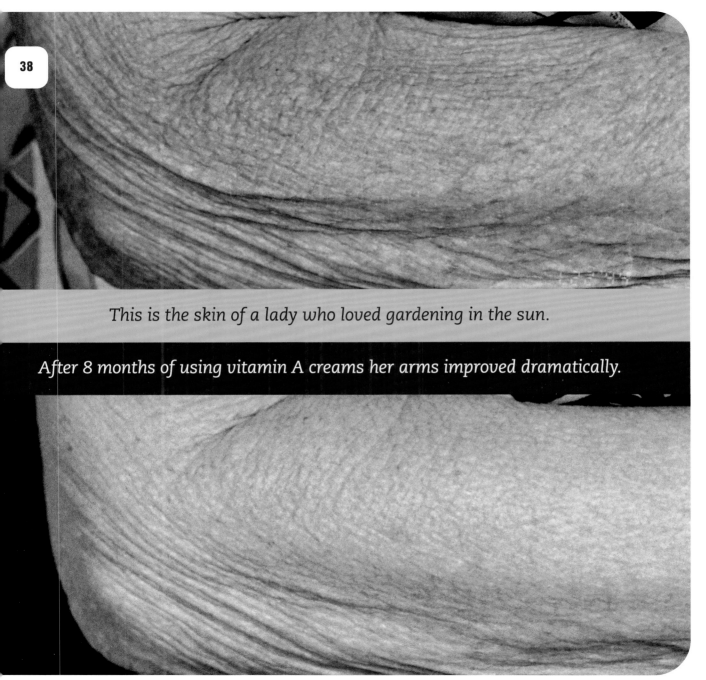

This is the skin of a lady who loved gardening in the sun.

After 8 months of using vitamin A creams her arms improved dramatically.

"

THE EFFECT OF THIS KIND OF IMPROVEMENT ON THE INDIVIDUAL WITH PHOTO-DAMAGE PIGMENTATION IS REMARKABLE!

"

When free radicals damage the Keratinocytes, pigmentation problems can occur.

Antioxidant creams make a big difference!

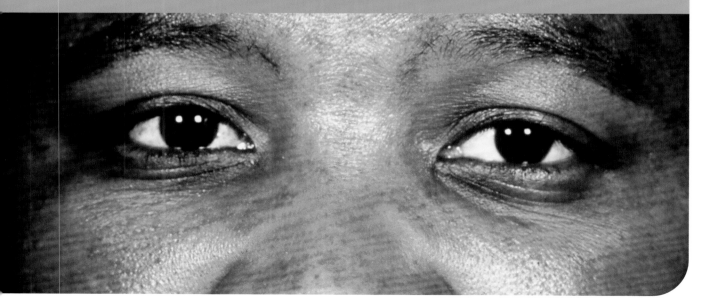

"

PIGMENTATION CAN BE GREATLY IMPROVED EVEN WHEN IT IS CAUSED BY HORMONES

"

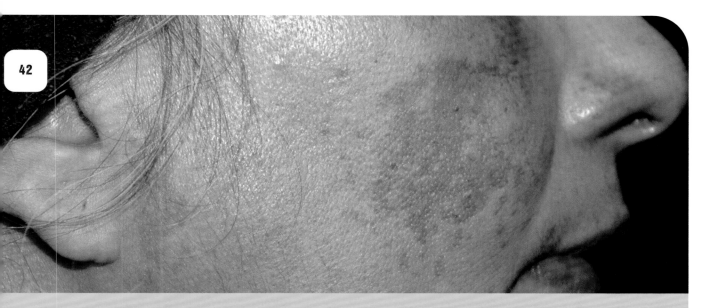

Pregnancy hormones caused this pigmentation.

Vitamin A created this difference!

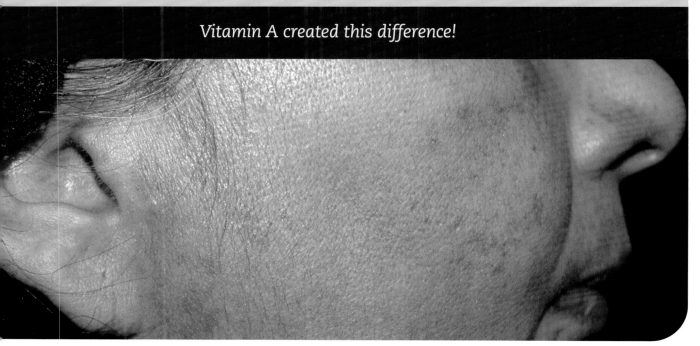

"REDNESS CAUSED BY PHOTO DAMAGE CAN BE VASTLY IMPROVED WITH VITAMIN A"

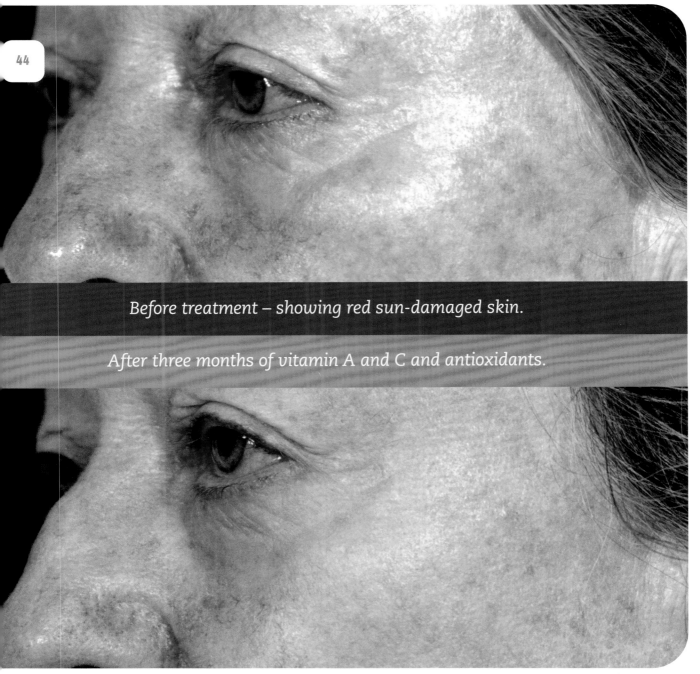

Before treatment – showing red sun-damaged skin.

After three months of vitamin A and C and antioxidants.

" EVEN SKIN CANCER RESPONDS FAVOURABLY TO VITAMIN A WHEN COMBINED WITH LIGHT SERIAL PEELS "

Vitamin A-rich skin DOES NOT get skin cancer!

A very, very good reason to keep your skin topped up with vitamin A – especially if you have pale Type i, ii or iii skin.

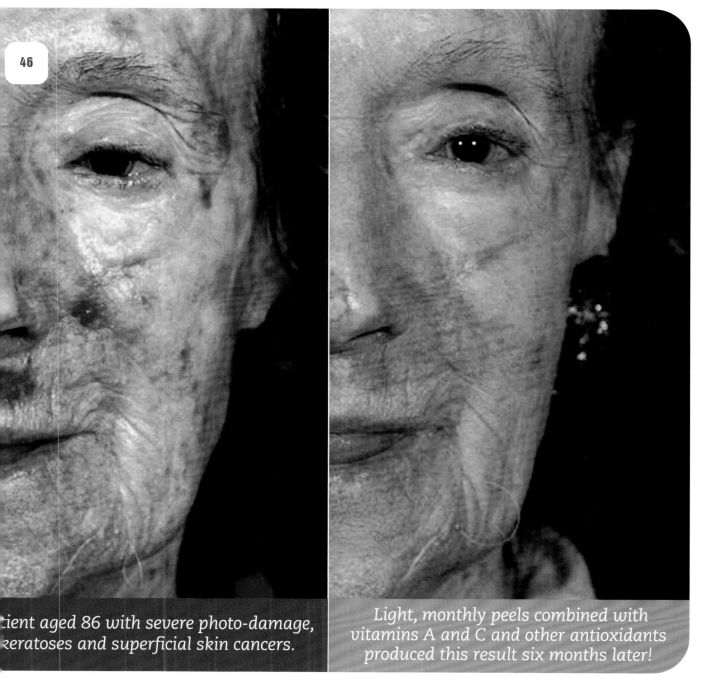

46

tient aged 86 with severe photo-damage, keratoses and superficial skin cancers.

Light, monthly peels combined with vitamins A and C and other antioxidants produced this result six months later!

© Environ

Dept #1. QUALITY CONTROL

"WHAT GOES **DOWN** CAN COME **UP** WITH **VITAMIN A**"

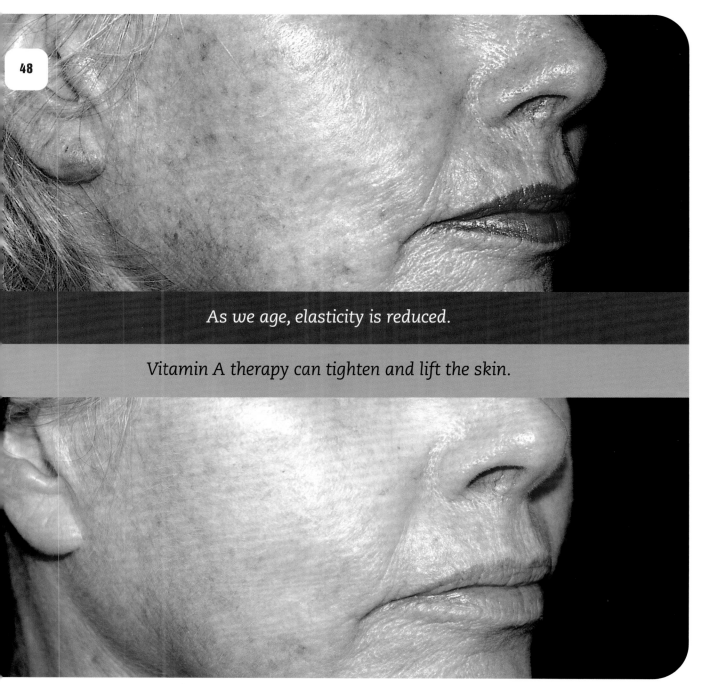

As we age, elasticity is reduced.

Vitamin A therapy can tighten and lift the skin.

VITAMIN A, OR DERIVATIVES OF IT, ARE GENERALLY USEFUL FOR PSORIASIS EVEN THOUGH IT DOES NOT CHANGE THE DISEASE – ONLY THE SURFACE APPEARANCE OF IT. VITAMIN A AND NEUTRALISED LACTIC ACID ARE VERY EFFECTIVE IN SMOOTHING THE SKIN.

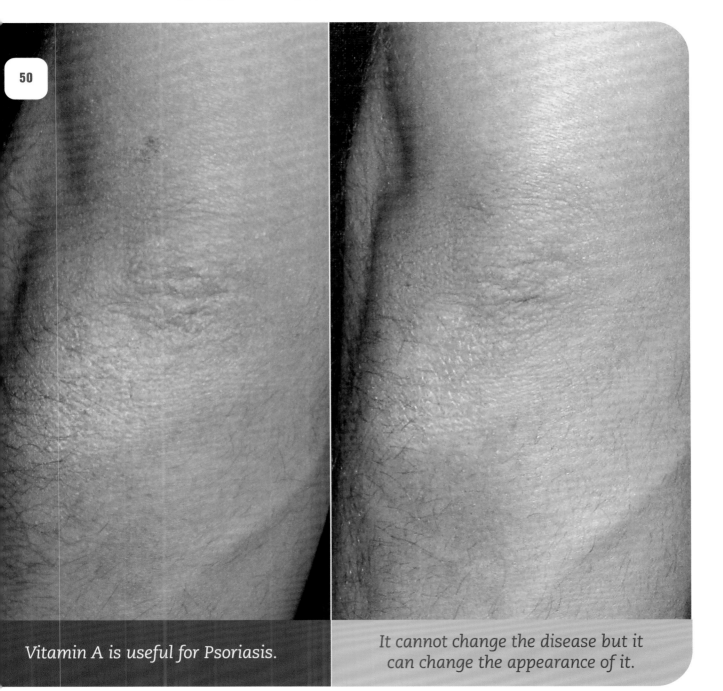

50

Vitamin A is useful for Psoriasis.

It cannot change the disease but it can change the appearance of it.

© Environ

"THE MISERY CAUSED BY ACNE CAN BE ALLEVIATED WITH VITAMIN A"

Vitamin A plays an important role in the treatment of acne, either as an oral supplement such as cisretinoic (Roaccutane or oral vitamin A), or as a topical application of retinoic acid, retinol retinaldehyde or retinyl palmitate. The higher the level, the more effective against acne – *but be careful to step up the level slowly to avoid a retinoid reaction.*

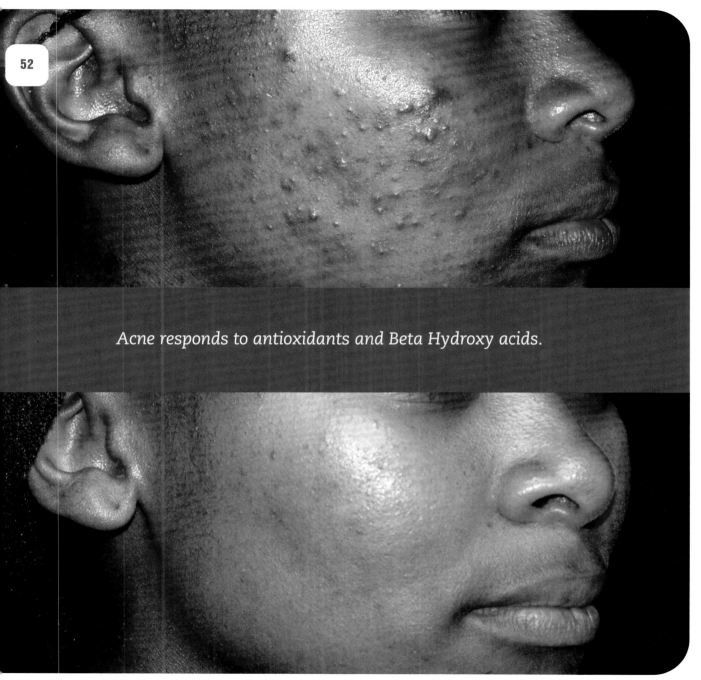

Acne responds to antioxidants and Beta Hydroxy acids.

Q.

WHY DO SKIN FACTORIES PRODUCE DEFECTS?

RELIABLE
FIRE ALARM
SPRINKLER ALARM

A.
SECURITY BREACHES
(and the damage they cause)

A.
POOR RAW MATERIALS
(and poor delivery of good raw materials due to damage)

Also: *Hormone activity, injury, disease*

Q.

AFTER SECURITY IS BREACHED AND DAMAGE CAUSED, HOW CAN YOU NORMALISE YOUR SKIN FACTORY AGAIN?

A.

IMPROVE DELIVERY
OF VITAMIN A
(and other raw ingredients)

THROUGH THE
BASEMENT
(Primary delivery bay – Epidermis)

AND
THE SHOWROOM
(Alternative Receiving Bay – Horny layer)

Q. WHAT IS A SECURITY BREACH?

A.

FREE RADICALS from pollution cigarette smoke and UV rays mess with the DNA plan, so that the factory gets colours and textures wrong.

UV DAMAGE TO LANGERHANS CELLS

When the Health and Safety Officer / Security Manager is damaged by UV rays he cannot perform his duties. Free Radicals sneak into the factory undetected, and without sufficient life-giving vitamin A the officer in charge of protection is inactivated!

  Smoking

 Pollution

 *UV rays*

"PHOTO-AGEING

(sun damage)

IS THE

EARLIEST PHASE

OF A

DISEASE

THAT LEADS TO

PIGMENTATION DISORDERS AND

SKIN CANCER"

*Dr Fernandes has believed
this for thirty years*

"ONCE SKIN HAS BEEN ENCOURAGED TO ACCEPT **VITAMIN A** THROUGH THE **'NORMALISATION'** PROCESS IT IS POSSIBLE TO **REPAIR DAMAGE** AND **PROMOTE GROWTH**"

"HOW TO LOOK AFTER YOUR BEAUTIFUL SKIN"

Dear Skin Factory Manager,

The most important thing to remember is that vitamin A (either in supplements or topically) is irreplaceable for the skin. There is simply no alternative for healthy skin at a cellular level. Many other expensive products will make your skin 'feel better', but nothing else will actually give you better skin. After many years of research and tests I am convinced of the truth of this.

Sincerely,
Dr Des Fernandes

Calendars +

Day

Mon Tue Wed Thu Fri Sat S

Every day event

Maintenance schedule for good skin

07:00

- Wash the face with simple water
- Apply your vitamin creams (A, C, E)
- Apply sunscreen
- Apply make-up if you choose – some make-up includes a sun-screen – bonus!
- Face the world!

The skin of the body requires vitamin A as much as the face.

Mix a little vitamin A oil or vitamin A body cream with some neutralised Alpha Hydroxy Acid and rub it all over the body; morning and night. That way you are hydrating and smoothing the skin and fuelling the factory all at once. Don't forget to rub sunscreen on all exposed areas, even if you sit in an office all day. UVA rays are still operating through the window panes and from artificial light and damaging your DNA!

22:00

- If you have used make-up, then pre-cleanse the skin with an oil-based pre-cleanser to remove it. This is also excellent if your skin is dry.
- Remove eye make-up with an eye make-up remover on a pad of cotton wool – be gentle!
- Cleanse with a cleanser appropriate for your skin. Remove with water or cotton wool – as you prefer.
- Use a toner but avoid an alcohol-based one unless necessary.
- Apply your vitamin creams as well as any repairing serums you need such as Colostrum or Retinol or serums to control pigmentation.
- If your skin is dry apply a hydrating oil.
- Sweet dreams!

No. 1
VITAMIN A

Internally and externally.

No. 3

SUNSCREEN

Always wear sensible sunscreen or creams enriched with antioxidants when exposed to damaging UV light.

No. 2
SUN PROTECTION

Reduce your exposure to the sun and always wear clothes that can protect you from the sun, especially hats. This is more effective than sunscreen.

No. 4

STAY AWAY FROM SUNBEDS

They can be worse than the sun!

No 5.
DON'T SMOKE OR BREATHE POLLUTION

No 6.
EAT WELL

No 7.
SLEEP WELL

No 8.
STRESS LESS

SPECIAL DELIVERY OF RAW MATERIALS

Once 'normalised', your Skin Factory will have a problem in receiving its deliveries of vitamin A – it becomes less permeable as it gets healthier!

Under normal conditions, in **healthy skin** all nutrients come through the **blood** BUT the skin has to share with all the **other organs** so cannot get enough. That is why **low doses of oral vitamin A** are of no great value to the skin.

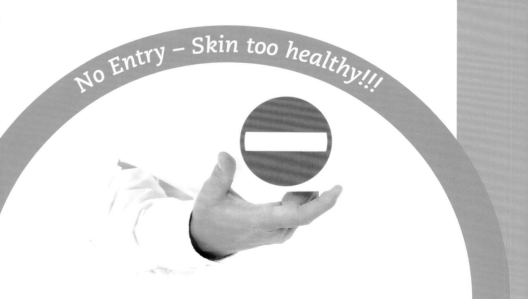

No Entry – Skin too healthy!!!

Your Skin Factory may need some help with penetration...

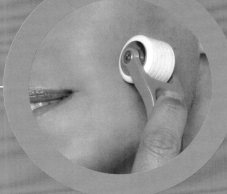

ADVANCED SKIN PERFUSION
makes tiny holes in the Horny layer to allow creams down into the lower level.

D.I.Y

IONTOPHORESIS
A galvanic current from a DF Ionzyme machine makes pathways down to the lower levels.

EXPERT

SONOPHORESIS
Sound waves from a DF Ionzyme machine make much larger pathways down to the lower levels.

EXPERT

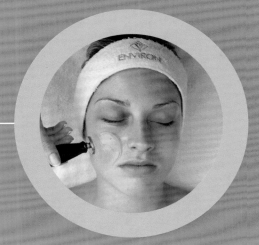

OVERHAULING THE FINAL PRODUCT

Peels

Peeling can help to aid penetration, and smooth photo-damaged skin; however light repetitive peels are preferable to torturous heavy ones.

A light touch is all you need

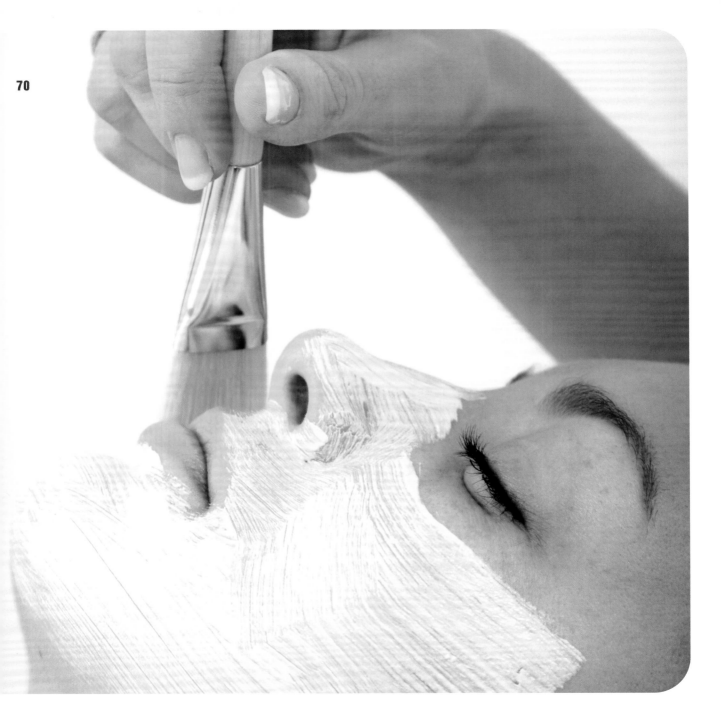

"EVEN OLD SCARS RESPOND WELL TO IMPROVED PENETRATION OF RAW MATERIALS"

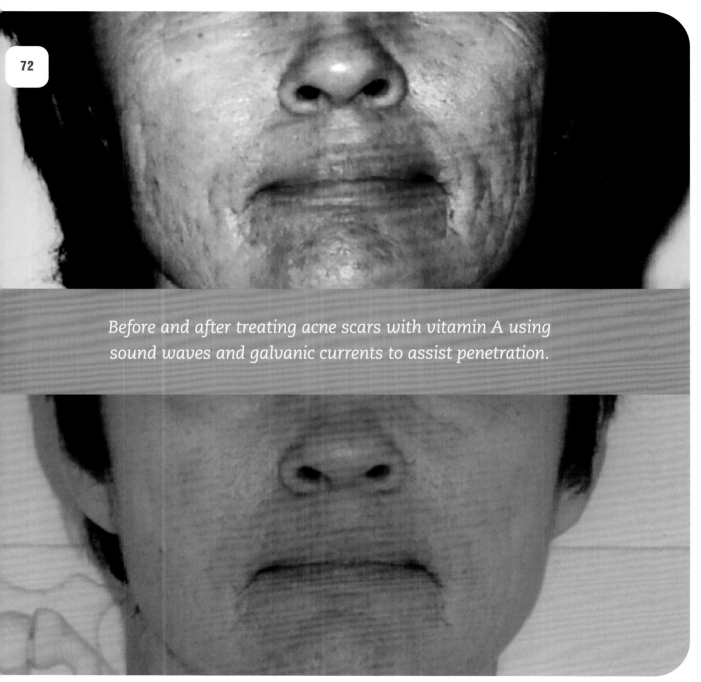

Before and after treating acne scars with vitamin A using sound waves and galvanic currents to assist penetration.

"
SCARS ARE NOT
IRREPARABLE

THEY CAN BE
IMPROVED BY
SPECIAL DELIVERY
OF **VITAMINS**
A & C
"

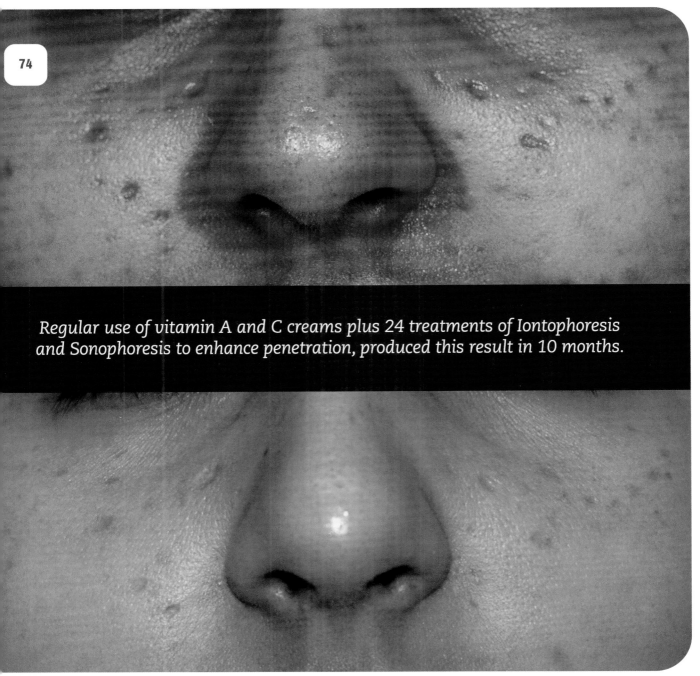

Regular use of vitamin A and C creams plus 24 treatments of Iontophoresis and Sonophoresis to enhance penetration, produced this result in 10 months.

"**SCARRED FOR LIFE** IS A **THING** OF THE **PAST!**"

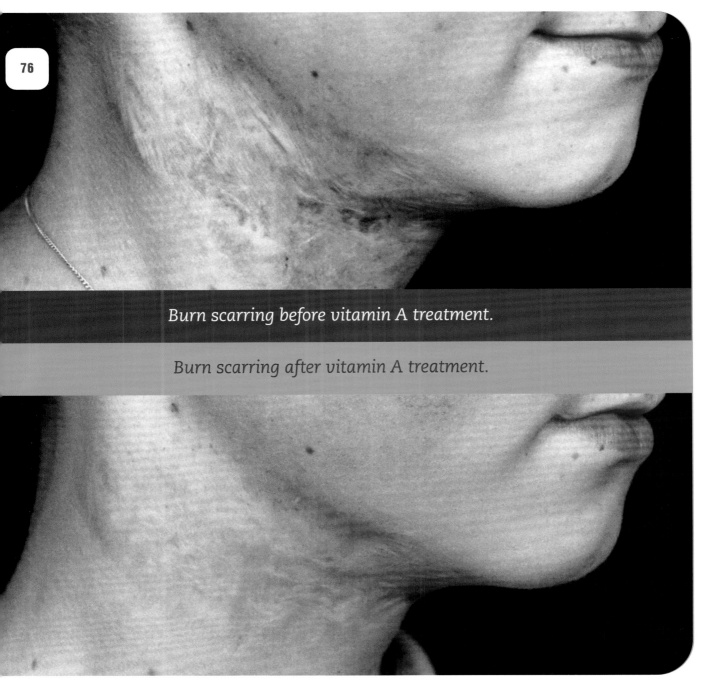

Burn scarring before vitamin A treatment.

Burn scarring after vitamin A treatment.

"AGEING SKIN IS NOT INEVITABLE

DAMAGE CAN BE REVERSED "

Before treating the skin of the neck.

After treating the neck with vitamin A using low frequency
sound waves and galvanic currents to assist penetration.

"LIGHTENING CREAMS CAN CAUSE DAMAGE WHICH IS REPAIRED BY VITAMIN A"

Vitamin A even improves this condition.
Even though the pigmentation has not been drastically
improved, the skin has been normalised sufficiently to
allow special active agents to perform properly.

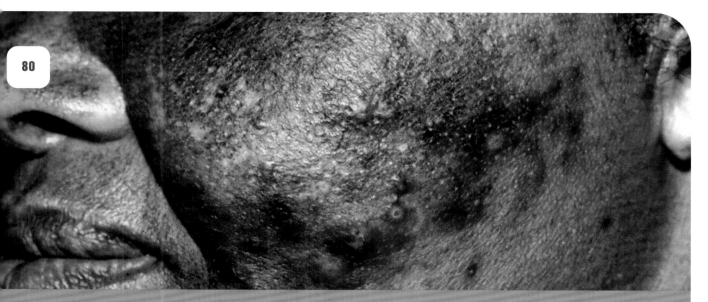

Chronic use of skin lightening agents often causes a condition called Ochronosis.

After six months use of vitamin A and antioxidants.

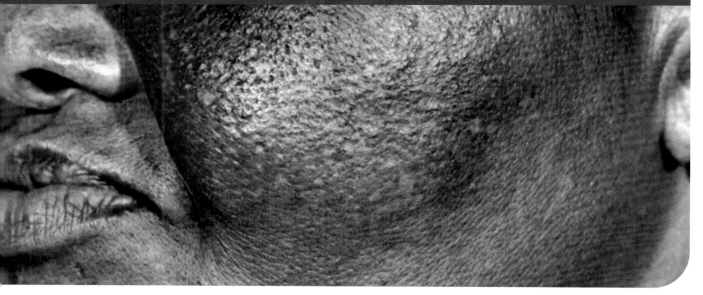

LUXURY MODEL

A VERY SPECIAL DEPARTMENT!

As a lizard grows a new tail, so your Skin Factory **can be changed by special techniques** to produce a completely new piece of the factory!

MEDICAL / SURGICAL

3.0 mm

Medical needles

Your Skin Factory

Percutaneous Collagen Induction Therapy

A NOTE FROM DOCTOR FERNANDES:

"Skin needling or Advanced Skin Perfusion is a treatment I invented and researched.

"If you prick the skin you also prick some blood vessels, and that causes a minor bleed. By bleeding you release platelets; the platelets assist in clotting the blood. They also contain growth factors which are designed to help injured skin heal rapidly. When we have pricked the skin we do not have an open wound, but these growth factors help to make skin thicker and more elastic and to develop more Collagen. That tightens up lax skin, smoothes out scarred skin and can even regenerate much more normal skin.

"The changes depend on the treatment being intensive enough, and to ensure the right level of intensity without the problem of being unsightly for a few days, it is necessary to do lighter treatments once a week for at least six treatments. Six light treatments would make as many holes in the skin as one intensive treatment".

DEPT #5. POST-PRODUCTION Repairs & Improvements
INTENSIVE

Pre-operation with 3mm needles and applying vitamin A and other raw ingredients.

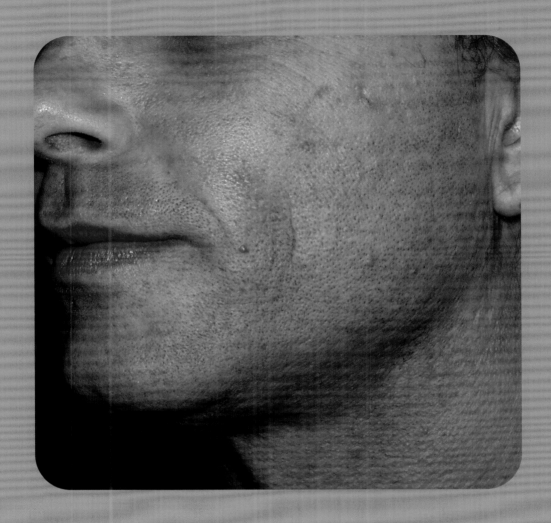

Two Years later!

"**SKIN NEEDLING USES THE BODY'S NATURAL RESPONSE TO INDUCE REGENERATION INSTEAD OF SCAR FORMATION**"

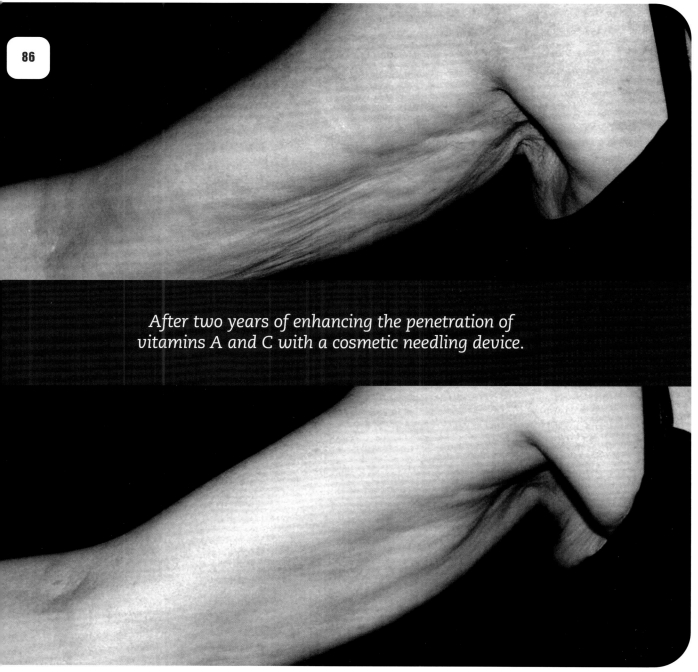

After two years of enhancing the penetration of vitamins A and C with a cosmetic needling device.

Dr. Des Fernandes

AN APPOINTMENT WITH THE DOCTOR / CO-AUTHOR

QUESTION:

What do you see as your mission in life?

ANSWER:

I've always wanted to help people to have the best skin possible. I'm outraged sometimes by how much hype surrounds normal cosmetic creams and how little they actually do for the skin. I saw it as my mission, some years ago, to create honest products and treatments that would really change the skin at a cellular level; things that could make it actually be better – not just feel better.

I'm interested in the science of skin, the health of skin and the well-being of the individual. I want to relieve the pain that people feel when they face scarring, acne, ageing and other dangerous or disfiguring skin problems.

Since two of my young patients died of melanoma, I've wanted to fight that disease and prevent it from destroying people's lives.

QUESTION:

When you formulated your products what did you do to make them different from normal cosmetics?

"**PEOPLE DON'T REALISE THAT THEIR AGEING SKIN IS A DIRECT RESULT OF SUN-INDUCED VITAMIN A DEFICIENCY.**

CORRECT THE DEFICIENCY AND YOU CAN HEAL AND REPAIR THE SKIN."

Dr. Des Fernandes

ANSWER:

I formulated them to deal with chemical changes that are induced by light, atmospheric pollutants, and the progress of time. I included doses of vitamins far higher than any other cosmetic products. This made the products difficult to manufacture and distribute, but I had no interest in making anything that wouldn't be effective. Even though it meant the product had to be manufactured under special conditions, and distributed through trained therapists only, I made the decision to do so because it was the only ethically correct way to proceed. Money was never my goal – healthy skin was my priority.

QUESTION:

Do you feel you now have the perfect product and you can leave it at that?

ANSWER:

Not at all! I am continually researching better ways to penetrate the skin, better formulations, new ingredients and better packaging. I am working on a facelift in a bottle that I hope will revolutionise the way we treat ageing skin. I am continually trialling the products and adjusting them as new discoveries come to light. The way ahead contains many exciting new ideas and inventions.

"**I want to make something that makes the skin actually be better —**

not merely feel or appear better."

Dr. Fernandes 1989

QUESTION:

What achievement are you most proud of?

ANSWER:

The pictures in this book show how vitamin therapy, properly applied in correct doses, can help people improve their skins to feel better, look better and actually be better. This is what I am most proud of.

In addition, I am very proud of the work I did when inventing the idea of a roller to make tiny temporary holes in the skin to allow the penetration of vitamin A and other antioxidants – Skin Needling or Advanced Skin Perfusion.

I introduced three different sizes of needles, and the deeper-penetrating ones can actually make skin rejuvenate itself. When I first reported on the long-term effects of Advanced Skin Perfusion no one believed me, and I have been thrilled to confirm that my methods were the first intervention in the history of medicine that caused regeneration and not scar formation.

> **Growth factors help to make skin thicker and more elastic and to develop more Collagen.**
>
> *Dr. Fernandes*

QUESTION:

What exactly is Advanced Skin Perfusion?

ANSWER:

Advanced Skin Perfusion is a treatment I invented and researched. If you prick the skin, you also prick some blood vessels, and that causes a minor bleed. By bleeding you release platelets, and the platelets normally assist in clotting the blood. They also contain growth factors which are designed to help injured skin heal rapidly. When we have pricked the skin we do not have an open wound, but these growth factors help to make skin thicker and more elastic and to develop more Collagen. That tightens up lax skin, smoothes out scarred skin and can even regenerate much more normal skin. However, the changes depend on the treatment being intensive enough. The problem is that if you have an intensive treatment then you will look unsightly for a few days, so I decided that we should do lighter treatments once a week for at least six treatments. I reckoned that with six light treatments we would make as many holes in the skin as in one intensive treatment. We often do these treatments at weekly intervals, and patients can go back to work within hours after the treatment.

Dr Des Fernandes MB, BCH, FRCS (Edin) – age 70

is a practicing plastic surgeon within the prestigious Renaissance Clinic in Cape Town. The experience of losing two young patients to melanoma 35 years ago, prompted him to uncover ways to help you to make your own beautiful healthy skin. Vitamin therapy was the result of his extensive research.

Jennifer Munro – age 57

is an author and writer, with a background in marketing and advertising. Jennifer is one of Des's early guinea pigs, and the way her own skin responded to vitamin A magic over the years made her want to write 'Your Skin Factory' with him.